Pep and Ben

By Cameron Macintosh

Pam can see Ben and Pep.

Ben can see Pep.

Pep can see the mat.

Ben sits at the mat.

Ben bit the mat.

Rip, rip, rip!

Pam has pet mats.

A set!

Pep and Ben sit.

CHECKING FOR MEANING

1. Who bit Pep? *(Literal)*

2. What happened to the mat? *(Literal)*

3. Why do you think Ben bit the mat? *(Inferential)*

EXTENDING VOCABULARY

bit	Look at the word *bit*. Can you think of other words that rhyme with *bit*?
rip	Look at the word *rip*. What sounds can you hear? Which sound is changed to turn *rip* into *rap*?
set	What do you think the word *set* means when Pam has a *set* of pet mats?

MOVING BEYOND THE TEXT

1. How do you think Pep and Ben feel about each other? Why?

2. How would the story be different if Pep and Ben didn't have a mat each to sit on?

3. Can you think of a real-life situation where you felt like Pep after Ben ripped his mat?

SPEED SOUNDS

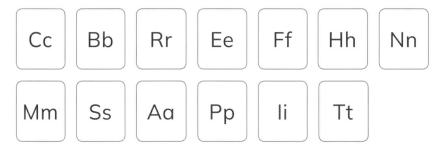

| Cc | Bb | Rr | Ee | Ff | Hh | Nn |

| Mm | Ss | Aa | Pp | Ii | Tt |

PRACTICE WORDS

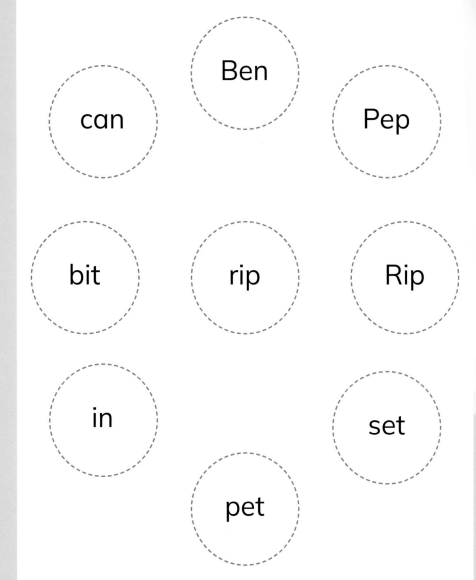

can

Ben

Pep

bit

rip

Rip

in

set

pet